D0999319

Also by Eleanor Lerman

Come the Sweet By and By (1975)
Armed Love (1973)

THE
MYSTERY OF METEORS

POEMS
Eleanor Lerman

Sarabande  Books
LOUISVILLE, KENTUCKY

Managing Editor
Sarabande Books, Inc.
2234 Dundee Road, Suite 200
Louisville, KY 40205

LIBRARY OF CONGRESS CATALOGING-IN-PUBLICATION DATA

Lerman, Eleanor, 1952–
    The mystery of meteors : poems / by Eleanor Lerman.
    p. cm.
    ISBN 1-889330-54-X (cloth: alk. paper) — ISBN 1-889330-55-8 (pbk: alk. paper)
I. Title.
PS3562.E67 M9 2001
811'.54—dc21   00-041309

Cover: *Comet Hale-Bopp*, by Ron Dawes. Image provided courtesy of the photographer.

Cover and text design by Charles Casey Martin.

Manufactured in the United States of America.
This book is printed on acid-free paper.

Sarabande Books is a nonprofit literary organization.

Funded in part by a grant from the Kentucky Arts Council, a state agency of the
Education, Arts and Humanities Cabinet, and by a grant from the National
Endowment for the Arts.

TABLE OF CONTENTS

THE MYSTERY OF METEORS

THE MYSTERY OF METEORS

I am out before dawn, marching a small dog through a meager park
Boulevards angle away, newspapers fly around like blind white birds
Two days in a row I have not seen the meteors
though the radio news says they are overhead
Leonid's brimstones are barred by clouds; I cannot read
the signs in heaven, I cannot see night rendered into fire

And yet I do believe a net of glitter is above me
You would not think I still knew these things:
I get on the train, I buy the food, I sweep, discuss,
consider gloves or boots, and in the summer,
open windows, find beads to string with pearls
You would not think that I had survived
anything but the life you see me living now

In the darkness, the dog stops and sniffs the air
She has been alone, she has known danger,
and so now she watches for it always
and I agree, with the conviction of my mistakes.
But in the second part of my life, slowly, slowly,
I begin to counsel bravery. Slowly, slowly,
I begin to feel the planets turning, and I am turning
toward the crackling shower of their sparks

These are the mysteries I could not approach when I was younger:
the boulevards, the meteors, the deep desires that split the sky
Walking down the paths of the cold park
I remember myself, the one who can wait out anything

So I caution the dog to go silently, to bear with me
the burden of knowing what spins on and on above our heads

For this is our reward: Come Armageddon, come fire or flood,
come love, not love, millennia of portents—
there is a future in which the dog and I are laughing
Born into it, the mystery, I know we will be saved

IN THE NEW SCHOOL

I know the story, but tell it again. Go on. Tell how, eons ago, epochs,
      you were tall and beautiful
Actors wanted you to phone them. Models left the runways
      to follow you home
and all their limousines waited outside while you slept alone,
      like a shimmering pearl in a silver shell
yet through all this, you somehow remained an innocent, an optimist—
      feverish even when you weren't sick
but that's because every night you went to school with angels
and they read you *La Chanson de Roland*, they read you stories in
      Greek and Latin
and let you run wild in the pharmacy. Oh boy, there were
marble halls and many mansions and motorcycles and zen
      and crystals and karma
and Katmandu and Number Nine, Number Nine, Number Nine
But that was in the old school, which I hear now has been closed—
      at least to you

So now you must attend the new school to make up for all your fun
You must start by getting down to fighting weight, which will be easy,
      since you won't be fed
And since your bones will ache, you must remove them all for examination
      though there is no timetable for when they will be returned
And you will learn nothing in the new school. There will be no lessons,
      no classes, no friends, no sex
You are just supposed to sit and think. That's why the chairs are so hard
That's why they've taken the glass out of the windows: a cold wind
      from a dead forest

will keep you from ever falling asleep again. How long
    does this go on?
What do they want from you? What do they want you to do?

Well, no one really knows. But here's a suggestion:
Write this in a note to the proctor and he will take it
    to whoever is running this place:
Tell them that you're sorry, you were mistaken. Tell them
that you were young so you didn't know, that you were in love
    so you were stupid
Tell them anything, tell them the truth. Tell them you'll be better
    when you're older
and though you're old already, remember—they are, too. So maybe
    they will understand your problem,
offer a solution, like to trade everything you ever wanted for everything
    you think you could live through now
And if you take it (we all take it) they will call this bargain, *mercy*
and they will tell you that you've graduated, they will (ha ha)
    let you go

THE BOOK OF WHAT IS IN THE DUAT

At the time of the First Occasion, which they later called
Zep Tepi, the jackal-headed god stepped into a boat of reeds
and sailed the winding waterway into another realm
Where shall we seek him now, our twin, our shadow soul?

Not in mighty Constantinople, nor in Rome
Not with the Jews, though they are constant
Not with the knights of Christ, though they still search
Not in obsidian, uranium, gold or lead or diamond
Not in the desert or the forest, not in the east or in the west
Not in the equinox or at the solstice, and not in what we dream

Not even in our prayers. For what could we ask?
To be desired? To be saved from pain?
To be led up to the mound wherein creation
has been rooted and dig down into the root, to the turtle
that rides the crocodile that prowls the galleries of fire
that are the shadow of the sunset and the mirror of the dawn?
Open *The Book of Going Forth into the Day*
and it will simply tell you to go forth
The jackal-headed god will meet you if he chooses
He will send no message if he does not

Now open *The Book of What Is in the Duat* and it will tell you,
Go down to any sky. Thus is the afterlife established:
it could be anywhere—above you or around you,
in the balance of the weight between a feather and a heart
In the Hall of Double Truth, there is nothing to believe

and no beloved: just you, swimming thought a night
bejeweled with starfish, to a mystery kingdom on another shore

FLORA STREET

for T. E. Lawrence

Now that I know what love is
I understand why it had to be given a wild horse and a
         white djellabah
and sent out, howling across the desert, to win a war
That is its place, I think, at the head of raging armies,
         planning battles, setting out on quests
or it should be locked up in a spice box and given to a king
Let love be immortal, let love make the king immortal,
let him be holy and pure and born again in madrigals and poems
Or let love manifest itself in archeology, let it be a
revelation on the road to Petra, an incantation carved on
         a Hittite shard
Or let it streak across the sky in incandescence, ten thousand
         years ago, ten thousand years from now
Let love define us. Let it burn

And now that I know what love is
I understand why it had to be punished in a cottage on a heath
         for turning back into its human form
I understand why it had to be outrun, outraced, why
         it had to be called by another name
And so I will not object when love is defiled
When it is unburied, buried all across the world,
when its finest robes turn out to be rags, its lovers, liars
         its mythology, suspect, its kindest act, rape
when it cannot walk without stumbling, speak without
         screaming, when it cannot

embrace without thinking about murder, lust, jealousy, revenge,
        I will take no action, nor will I be surprised
Let love struggle in vain. Let it be damned

And then . . . let it return
Because even now that I know what love is
        and has been and will be
I still remember you on Flora Street. It is summer;
there is music from someone's radio and church bells
        ringing in the distance
You are standing on the corner, holding a box of bakery cookies
and you—your heart, being, kisses, body and bone—you are
        waiting for me
And that alone may be enough to stay the hand of banishment,
to journey out to where love wanders in its white djellabah,
        innocent and arrogant,
posing itself against the setting sun. And though its terms remain
        forever unacceptable,
its promises broken before they are even made, you alone,
alive in me in memories of Flora Street, may be the reason
        to pretend I have seen nothing
as love, in its finery or tatters, slips back into the world

THE FARM IN WINTER

—Trumansburg, New York, 1969

Cold ponies in the fields, rows of pumpkins
ready to volunteer themselves into pies
Ice on the road has made a road of silver arrows;
last night the moon flew through the sky
like a silver arrow flying true through winter
Everything is sharp and dangerous: it will
be a challenge just to go buy bread
I should be telling you every minute, every
minute, that this is the happiest I have ever been

This is what I look like on the way to town:
two sweaters, the farmer's old boots, and
an anorak with a French label (because style
is still important, even out here in the farmland)
Ravens follow me down the lanes between
lonely pine trees, lonely timber; only the firs
have stayed alive for Christ and Christmas
I am walking on the graves of last year's
vegetables; next year's peppers, green and
indomitable, rattle in their sleep

On Main Street I buy nails and biscuits
Later, at the crossroads (where north
will take you to the Berkshires, deeper into
winter, into snow), someone stops to ask,
How is the harpsichord maker? as if
you were already grown old into your craft

And in my mind there comes a picture of you:
lean and skillful, born ten times into magical
generations of yourself, a creator, who rescues
wood from the growing seasons and teaches it
to serve, harmoniously, the more eternal seasons
of music. And I am going home to you and your
mystical tools: the plane, the saw, the plectrum

and I am going home to you, in the long ago,
in the time before everything, on a perfect day

WILD WIND, GREEN TEA

Your birthday. A dark night of wild wind and goblin clouds
The moon rocks in starry rafters, yellow lanterns sizzle on the
terrace, which you've opened to the sky. You are delighted
with all this mad weather, with the witch dreams of October
Cold sheets, cold kisses, nightgowns dancing by themselves:
this is what a good soul conjures with wicked wishes, why
the world won't harm you, why it is yours. Why instead of
cake, there are little dishes of green tea ice cream, civilized
and pure. Yet also full of secrets, strange and tasty. You hold
out the spoon and say, *One bite and you are mine forever*
And because I believe you, I refuse that first mouthful, waiting
to gobble it all later, when I am ready to meet my fate

OFFICE IN A SMALL CITY

Edward Hopper, oil on canvas, 1953

A Chinese woman on the train is eating sugared almonds and
reading a book called *Information*. For weeks, I will be wondering
what the information could have been about. Here is a partial list
of my best guesses: How do you build a clavichord from a kit?
What is the weight of all nine planets? How do you contact
major celebrities? How do you breed small birds?

On a related subject, I know some people from Romania
Sometimes they sing a song that goes, *Romania, Romania*
They are also in need of lots of information. Here are some
of the things they need to know: What are the current rules
about immigration? What is the format for a business letter?
How do you plant a winter garden? Where are the best
places in this city to buy table wine and sturdy shoes?

My problems are a little different. I already know too much
for my own good. I have so much information that even my sleep
is agitated. Numbers, dates, computer code—they are onscreen
all the time. And do you hear the noise? I think it is the millennium
crunching data in the warehouses of the coming empire
where high tension wires will span the globe, cables will
electrify the ocean floor. We'll spin between the poles, between
the grid lines, hyper-conscious, full of knowledge, nearly insane

But for now, I am living in a painting. A man in shirtsleeves
sits at his desk, looking out the window at the mild sky above
a mild city, a small city with a clean river and manageable roads

He has no tasks, he has no supervisor. He believes a soldier
is the president, though he never votes. He doesn't remember
where he lives, or if he is married. He has no children, he has
no pets, no wishes or desires. He is filled with eternity
He is inevitable. He is perfect, silent, calm

I sit behind him sometimes. Sometimes I hand him a pen
He puts it down on the desk and goes back to gazing
at the quiet skyline. Later, in the blue hours of the evening,
the city turns in early. We, on the other hand, never sleep

Sometimes I am the man in the painting. I take his place
as the observer. Sometimes I think that the city below
is empty: machines make coffee, streetlights change
from red to green, from stop to go, but there are
no people to obey them. There never were
Sometimes I put my cheek to the window glass and can
feel the vibrations of the future, the wheels of the future
rumbling, an echo in the structure, in the steel

and sometimes I feel the future coming with its
immortal hunger and its lies

THE ALCHEMIST'S PRAYER

Perceval, now begins the time of thy last quest when we
must wait for thee at the edge of the great woods
      at the end of the world
And there we will guard for thee the white rose and the
red rose, which are the symbols of alchemical blending
and which are the intertwining of the heart of Jesus and
      his mother's tears
And as well, so will we guard for thee the great fish
Leviathan, keeping him safe in the deep well of our
unconscious yearning until, with grail and lance, Perceval,
      return to us
and make of him redemption, the meal of all humanity
We wait, son, savior, knight. Go and find the castle
      and the king

whose surname is called dragon. For he is ill and when
the king is ill the land is ill, ruled by the dark, uncanny
      nature of the moon
So go thee, Perceval, into the forest and ask the old, lame king:
Who serves the Grail? To whom does it belong? Ask for the
world above and the world below, and for all the spirits
      lost, lost, lost between
Ask for the souls to whom knowledge is denied and thus
      salvation is denied
Ask for us and be for us the seven battalions, the holy aspects
      of eleven, the embodiment of Trinity

that gave a boy the strength to pull the sword out of the stone
And on thy quest, do not become bewitched by maidens, be pure,
      follow the signs,
and listen for angels' voices in the smoke and in the mist
Recognize when thou hast entered the psychic regions, the place
      of dangerous transition
Obey thou the lion if he command thee in the forest, but slay
the giant and trust no other knight, be he on horse or alone,
      on foot
Rely on nothing but thy inner goodness and thy compassion and
reconcile, thee, Perceval, to thy ascension to the Fisher's throne,
for in this way shall God be reconciled with Nature, Arthur
      wakened from his dream of Avalon,
and thy people and thy country freed from devastation by thy
      human hand and in thy human name

THE LESSON OF THE QUEEN

The queen is unhappy. And why not? She is trapped
in the 11th century, in all those difficult clothes
The roads are stony, the food is poor, and when she's ill
a madwoman rushes in to diagnose distemper
Amputate! Amputate! That's all the surgeons know
Her children plot against her, her equerries are thieves
The queen longs to leave this cold country
and walk all the way to Asia, wherever that may be
Meanwhile, war is rumored with the lowlands, with
the soldiers of the church. She will lose her horses and
all her money. She knows that she will never get away

But in our time, things are better: we have awakened
to a perfect New York Sunday: May, flags flying,
what you in your slim pajamas call Marlo Thomas weather,
bringing boyfriends, trips to Bonwit's, every flower
Monet every painted blooming by the roads. And so we dress,
we drive into the city, have an English breakfast—jam and
apricots—at a café in the park. (We are playing with the city,
experiencing our culture: all this is what we're meant to do)
Blocks away, in a museum, there is a bone, a comb, a dull jewel
in a reliquary, last home to Gertrude, Mary, Boadacia, Ragnhild,
Thyra, Jane. Poor queen. Even the emeralds in her crown were grim

If we look back, what can we learn from that woman
brooding deep in history? Imagine what, if we visited
her marrow and her tatters—that we are somehow connected
to her pain? We are not. We do not witness or inherit such

distant legacies: All women are not all women. When we
breathe, it is just possible that all we are creating is ourselves
So what can we learn? Perhaps the lesson is in the limits:
How human are we? Which connections will be broken?
Which promises will endure? For there are only so many
perfect Sundays, so many chances to see beyond the shadow
on the emerald to the lover in the café, the café in the morning,
the morning we are wedded to each other by the brief
but passionate ceremony that turns out to be our lives

REMOTE VIEWING

This is what we'll do: I'll go to Mexico and
       lie down on a sacrificial stone,
a big one, with lots of carvings: feathered beasts,
panthers chewing on unworthy hearts. You go
       to Soho, go to the galleries
Buy a small bronze statue, a piece of ormolu, the
       most expensive shoes you can find
Then meet your friends for drinks. Drink
       Cosmopolitans
Linger over the cherry—you know what to do

Then when the time is right, make an announcement
Explain that you have a lover in the jungle, a worried,
       unhappy person
who thought of nothing but doom all the way to the
       Distrito Federal
in the back of a bus. Go into a trance: say you
see me now clutching an emerald, say that I told you
       that if I drop the emerald,
the world as we now know it will come to an end

The question is not, do you echolocate, slip
       like smoke down the lines of latitude
or send up flares into an alternative sky—
       everyone knows
that you are capable of more. The question is,
       which one of us is the nice one?

Which one weeps for vengeance in the darkness,
which one counsels mercy while she plays for time?

THE STRANGE ATTRACTOR

Science has given us many ways to model instability
and to express the fragile state of systems experiencing
      erratic flux and flow
Here is mine, which you may think of as an abstract:
if I have the strength, I may present a more complete and
      annotated paper later on:

Because of an argument that takes place halfway up
      Cape Cod,
I find myself stranded in Barnstable, Massachusetts with
      only an overnight bag and my pills
(Please note: I am not the one who has the temper)
It's a nice town with a harbor famous for its sunsets
(which are often significant but also random: —sometimes
      ruby red, sometimes pale, weak,
grapefruit yellow; and sometimes, if the day is cloudy, they
      don't appear at all),
but since I hadn't planned on being here, I am unclear
      about my options
Should I wait around or try to hitchhike all the way
      to Provincetown?
Paralyzed by unpredictability, I buy a donut and some coffee
and sit down on the curb by Route 6A. I am staying, I am going
I am feeling the anxious edges of my own slow approach to
      all kinds of death

Now, what do you think of the story I just told you?
Do you think it really happened? For our purposes, it

doesn't matter:
If it hasn't happened yet, in time, it will. For our purposes,
we will attempt to study it. We can use a diagram called
        the Lorenz Attractor,
which is meant to help us understand the structure that
may exist where there appears to be no structure, where
forces are turbulent and disordered and running at a
        fever pitch
The attractor represents something we can cling to
        as we sip our coffee,
something we can brush crumbs from as we take our pills
We can draw it on a napkin or on the tablecloth—or preferably
        in blood (weak blood or ruby)
in the middle of Route 6A. But it won't help. No matter
how hard we persist in attempting to construct this diagram
the variables remain incomprehensible, the developing
        image, incomplete

So what do you think? Will the love of my life come
        back for me?
Deep in the fluid dynamics of that fibrillating heart
will the other, the strange attractor, finally exert itself?
Or in the end, will science fail me? Claim uncertainty
        and inconclusive evidence,
when what I need is mercy. And a plan

HYANNIS

Even if you just whisper, I will listen
Even just in passing, mention time and distance
      and I will look up from my work
drawn to hear it rumored once again: that there is
      one way left to follow
one moment after this one through which I may escape
So do not look for me. I will be traveling everywhere,
      in all directions
I will be living in the future and in the past
I will be anything you can imagine. A diving bird. A bolt
      rattling in the wind

Mention time and distance:
There are the yellow flowers in Hyannis. Blue shutters,
      white fences
Lawn chairs and linen and sunlight on the grass
Later, the only brother that I love dines with me in a restaurant
He chases away my boyfriends. He speaks to me in dreams
He is older, he is younger—he will survive everything that
      ever happens
He will draw maps on napkins. He will tell me how

Now I am living in the future and the past:
There is old age, which welcomes me
I will relax into these old bones. I will shake them out like
      broken diamonds
Rest them far from suffering and gall
And though centuries and storms assault my house,

it cannot be assaulted
for here I have outlasted wars. I have survived love

So do not try to stop me
I will always be traveling toward Hyannis
The only brother that I trust is driving
The roads are empty. In the villages, no one is home
No tides trouble the hidden heart
And even the deepest seas surrounding us are calm

A CALIFORNIA STORY

In the Simi Valley, in the back bedroom of a baby blue house
        sitting on a dusty lot, I am sitting on the bed
It's hot as blazes, it's later than it's ever been, it's darker
        than the dark side of the moon
The dog is sitting opposite me, panting for some water
or a walk. It is in this context, formed by bubbling blips
of information or sliding images that pop up on the brain screen
disguised as random human thought, that the question occurs:
What is the universe? Aha. An old one. A good one. Best of
        the west, top of the pops.
What is the universe? *Just work on that one for awhile,* the
neural network suggests before ceasing broadcast for the night

Well, I'll bite. Here is an easy answer: I can see part of it
        from the Valley
though more from the Holmby Hills (you get more of everything
        up where the movie stars live):
It's that vast Egyptian darkness seeded with pharaohs, that
churning, uncrossable river of stars and miles and light and milk—
        or maybe not
Maybe it's a state of mind (not mine, surely, but someone's)
or a province in the windy north. Maybe it's *maya.* Maybe
        it isn't
Maybe it's Jesus' pain. Or your pain. Maybe it's nothing
Maybe it's black and sparkly, or distorted by strange forces,
        maybe it goes on and on or is about to end
Maybe it's so unimaginable that you would panic if you
        knew the truth

26

Or maybe it's this: on a hot night in the Simi Valley,
a woman picks up a panting dog and puts it in her car
And then she drives along beautiful roads, California roads,
velvet roads that wind through velvet canyons down to
         the velvet sea
And when she gets there, she takes off her shoes and
picks up the dog, which she carries down to the water so
it can swim amid the starfish, in the cool waves
The dog thinks the woman is the nicest person in
         the universe, whatever that may be
The dog is in the ocean, the ocean is beneath the stars
Dog, star, universe: what are they, really? Manifestations
         of kindness and mystery in the Simi Valley?
Or just a California story containing a woman who knows
         what she regrets

THE OUTING

for Philip Lerman

It's a long trip, especially since I'm hiding a nineteen pound dog
in a carry bag; an agreeable animal who I'm pretending is a
collapsible beach umbrella. But when the train finally arrives
at the first station down the shore and the salt spray and the
crayon colors of the light (yellow, blue, sparkle green and
sparkle foam) spill into my heart, the journey is rewarded
Two stops later, I unfold the dog and we march up to the
boardwalk through such soft air! (These must be prewar
breezes, so innocent and serene.) Then we find a bench,
share a custard cone and I settle under my headphones to
listen to the ballgame crackling in from Boston, Baltimore,
Cleveland, Chicago or the Bronx. These are the best games,
the hardball of the old league, the old sooty cities and one
angry borough, where bats wave in the stands like the
collective defiance of the downtrodden, riveted into wood

July. Three o'clock in the afternoon. The Yankees are
up by two and I am at the beach. I could be my father.
I could be my own child. And this is the only plan I
have: that when I get too old to carry this dog, I'll buy
another, as tiny as a shell that I can hide in my shirt
pocket. And when I lift her to my ear I will hear the
wind blow and the ocean roar and life, life, life going on

DOMINION

We spent the night in Maryland, in an old house with stone floors
    and stairs as steep as a bookcase
An October landscape crouched outside the window: bent
    trees, low hills
Witch country, I told you. *No*, you said, *there were no witches
    in the slave states*
That didn't help. I went to sleep and dreamt about a woman
    who had something in her eye
She was given an operation, and when she woke up, she was dead
(This really was my dream.) I feel funny, she said to the nurses,
    but they wouldn't name the problem
Ha ha, you said, when I related this in the morning. *You really have
    been watching too much* TV

Then we drove on to Washington. A gray day in the capitol,
    though that hadn't stopped the crowds
Schoolchildren were touring the FBI building, nuns were lunching
    at the CIA
The Freedom of Information Act, I decided, had changed everything:
    the spooks, the sergeants
were all quick to grant us access: *These are your museums*, they
    pointed out
These are your files (Like every other mild paranoid my age,
    I believe I have a file
though I'm sure it's pretty flimsy. Someone like Patty Hearst,
    on the other hand,
probably has one a mile wide.) *There are still lots of secrets*

in these buildings, you reminded me
And I believe that. There are secrets everywhere. Secrets in us

Later, I wanted to see a famous building with walls converging
        in a famous point
that everyone has to touch, including me. It's like rubbing
the backbone of a beast, folding your hand along the spine
        of a sleeping world
Don't do it, you warned me, though I had said I would
        for weeks
It will only make you feel crazy. And you were right:
        for hours
I felt as if I had a soul, and that soul had mingled with
        a million ghosts,
a million handprints of the touring public. *I tell you and*
        I tell you, you sighed, *but you never listen*
All over the world, in every language, someone is saying that
        to someone else right now

Later, we drove on to Harper's Ferry. Sunlight made a
        dramatic entrance in the afternoon,
dropping thin golden shafts between still-threatening clouds
We parked the car and crossed a footbridge that led back
        a hundred years,
past flood markers and plaques commemorating John
        Brown's raids
On a steep street, in a shop that had been built before
        the Civil War
I stopped to buy a button from a soldier's uniform, lingering
        for a long time over my choice:
blue, because they saved the Union, or gray because
        you have to sympathize with tragedy?

In the end, of course, I bought them both. You bought
a map of the Chesapeake and sat on a stone wall
       eating ice cream,
planning the rest of our trip. I walked on, climbing
       a path to the Maryland Heights
and up there on the cliffs, buffeted by winds, by death,
       history, dreams, war, and information
I wondered, *Over what do I have dominion?* Don't think
       that even now I have a clue
though it was a reasonable question to ask in a place where
       I could see the convergence of two great rivers
but no further south, over the curve of the earth, to wherever
       they were going

TO MONTREAL

Enough already—why don't we just get in the car and drive?
That's what we did when we were younger:
Wake up in the middle of the night with a feeling of *let's go*
and head north, deep into winter, straight up 95,
right to the border and beyond. In those days, we could live on
one sandwich and half an ounce of hashish. But hurry now, hurry
I want to be cold in a French city. I want to go to Montreal

We'll shop. We'll buy shoes and dresses; furs
I'll call you *cherie*. We'll smoke cigarettes to achieve
a Russian look. We'll sleep in the finest hotel on rue Rachel
and when we rise, I will feed you cake and tea with cinnamon
Cherie. You are the heart of me. Like the living moon,
alive in early morning, you prove that we have put
the night behind us. That we have another day

Let's go to Montreal. We'll be closer to the pole star
We'll drink coffee and eat chocolate in a garden of ice and snow
I want to see you in boots and gloves walking on a cobbled street,
walking under colored lights with ice crystals in your hair. I want
to see you through the window of a gallery buying postcards
of frozen rivers, frozen lakes and icebound streams

So hurry now, hurry. While the stars are still out, while the
temperature is dropping, while true north pulls us toward
the Milky Way, let us steal off into the night. Tomorrow,
strangers will point us out on Catherine Street. They will say,

There are the lovers who came to see the northern lights
Welcome them into our city, into the home of the north wind

NIGHT FLIGHT

New York–Los Angeles 1999

I'm sitting on my luggage at two a.m., watching tired cops
       drink coffee
An air hostess from the Balkans (I can tell, I'm good at accents)
drags her weary self over to the telephones and tries to make
       a call to London
Good luck, little sister—even the microwaves are exhausted
Ping, ping, ping (that's me, imagining how radar sleeps)
Now Trude (I've named her) is crying as she tucks away her
       phone card
There's got to be a story there, but I'm too shaky to
       make friends
I'd have to frisk her for plastique, check her carry-ons
       for bullet holes
See? Already I'm imaging explosions in midair
But that's the danger of booking yourself an aisle seat
       on the red eye:
You begin to believe you'll have to live here, that they'll
       never call your flight

And what I really want is to be back in Opa-locka
To sit down, hard and heavy, on the banks of the muddy,
       blue-green Gulf
and release my paranoia. It would steam in the humidity,
       curl up like an old banlon shirt
and blow away. Instead, I'm sending it on a hop-skip
       to the source code,

programming for full anxiety after midnight, taking the
        night flight from New York to LA

I am too old for this, too old for emergencies; too old
        probably, for a private life of any kind
That's where the damage comes—from knowing
        strange people in strange businesses
They send coded messages to your e-mail, leave
money in your mailbox and tickets to oblivion at
        your front door
That's why I had to come up the Intercoastal, take a
        meeting on Mott Street
with old friends from Red Bank, on the Jersey side
Bad guys, bad guys. You think I'm kidding?
We're all too old for this, we're up too late at night
Too many airports, too many taxis: thirty dollars
        from Delancey,
thirty dollars to travel through the vapor glow at
        light speed,
to hunker down and buckle up, to do this one
        more time

And by the time we hit the Rockies, don't think
        I won't be sick
Don't think I won't feel the suck, the pull of that
blood-red electric coral aqua glow that starts at LAX
        and then proceeds to kill you
If I make it to bed by afternoon, I swear to sleep alone
Wowie zowie, kids and cuties. That's the sound of me
knowing much too much about what's not in the
        tourist guides to NYC, LA

Tornado Days

Up early in the raw morning, the dog and I go out to hunt the day
The dog—who would be a silly animal if I let her,
        too small to be ferocious—
is learning, at least, to be lean and silent. And I am learning
        to cover my tracks
This is how you prepare, when you don't know what is coming
This is how you start when you must leave everything behind

So we go out into a field of memories, down a path to a witch's house
in a time of no shields, in the plague time, the time without God
This is the child's time, when only a pariah dog can be tamed
        as a companion
But here is the next place: a river house, with great planked floors
Blue water and silver salmon rush by the open door as people
        dance and stomp across the floor
Hear the music, smell the water and the wind!
This was the time, the long ago, when I was in love

But these are not the things that we are hunting, the little wolf and I,
not now that we have entered the tornado days, the wild days,
        the days of such pain that we can't even bleed
Chained together, beast and ghost, we walk the dead streets,
        the dead hours, waiting for the next age to commence
This is what you do when you have nothing left
This is what you do when you are dying

So here is the last place: the days of lust and science,
        the killer days,

the worst days, the days that will experiment on you like Nazis
These are the days that I knew were coming: the days of signs
     and secrets
So I keep an animal with me to remember my faith,
a glimpse of love that can dance down the whirlwind
     and go out to hunt the wandering serpent
whose riddles must be answered before he dreams us all again

Missing Time

for Betty and Barney Hill

Five million Americans believe they have been abducted by aliens

They are loggers on a lonely road, lonely ballerinas in a city,
doctors, psychiatrists, people who like horses, friends, twins,
          children, comedians, interracial couples
They are never very fat. They are never old nor do they have
          unusual personalities
Not one has ever been a member of the Latin Kings

And this is what happens. Let's say, to you:
It's Friday. You and your brother are on your way
to bingo and you have packed extra colored markers
          in your bingo bag
(Your brother's wife has left him and you think maybe a night
          at the Indian casino will cheer him up)
You get in your car and travel a few miles but are soon
forced off the interstate by a detour, or because you forgot
          you needed gas
Then, driving along some winding country road (you know
          where this is going), your brother,
depressed as he is, looks up into the star-filled sky and says,
          Sweetie, what is that light?

Next thing you know, the two of you are sitting on the
          side of the road
Your head hurts and your arms are sore
It's four hours later and you are mystified by all that

missing time
Perhaps, you tell each other, you just fell asleep
But let me warn you what will happen: months later—
       maybe years—
you will be sending crazy postcards to Whitley Strieber
and weeping in the library when you see those
       grainy drawings of the little grays
You will be divorced, you will be screaming in your sleep
       and you will wonder,
What the hell is this all about? But like every other issue,
       event, problem, philosophy
or religious dilemma you have ever confronted, no one
will have a satisfactory answer or any useful information
       worth a good goddamn
And that's the way it is sweetie, that's just the way it is:
We're born, strange things happen that confuse us—
and to make it worse, maybe we're even born again

So get used to it, because this is how you will
       end your days:
confined to a dark room scratching star maps on the walls
       with a needle and a broken knife
After you're gone, astronomers will determine that you have
       charted an unknown galaxy
and celebrate your discovery with a plaque. But what good
       will it do you?
You'll be just another victim of space exploration,
while the cosmic dust you have become goes rattling
       around the universe, looking for
your brother, your colored markers, someplace quiet
       to call home

Hot Town, Sukiyaki

We are on the 37th floor of the RCA building and
we aren't feeling funny. This is a problem, since
NBC is paying us to write jokes. By midnight, we're
trying to convince each other that "dreaded wheat"
is a phrase that will make America laugh. Leaving
the office that we use at night, we start wandering
the halls, looking at pictures of the secretaries' cats
My mind is wandering, too: I am thinking about a
hat I saw that had bees and flowers made out of
green beads. The hat was in a shop in Brooklyn
called Glamorama, which is next door to Junior's
restaurant where we could get some of the best
cheesecake . . . well, see? I don't need to be reminded
that right now, a famous, angry, coked-up comic
is on the red-eye from L.A., hurtling towards us
at a million miles a minute—and when he gets here,
we can't just put him in a rabbit suit and push him
out on stage. We're Jews in show biz; we should
damn well be able to come up with something soon

An hour later, the comic is an hour closer (picture this:
sour and vicious, he is bumping through the rolling
clouds), while all we've been doing is pushing each other
down the corridors in a mail cart with a squeaky wheel
Connie, my partner, who is handsome and ambitious,
has called his agent twice. The agent is in Oxnard,
visiting his parents (we're still low-level talent; this is
all the representation we can get). But for once, the agent

has a good suggestion: write a sketch that will involve
the comic with the rock band that the show has booked
(picture this: they're out cold, they're flying Virgin in
from London, at least two of them will overdose within
a year). This will work, because all comics want to be
rock stars, and rock stars, if fed enough Kristal and
Quaaludes, will do anything you want. In twenty
minutes, the dialogue is written and Connie, standing
at the window, looking at the city, which is black and
magenta, which is the stage set of every movie, which is
brilliant and backlit and a labyrinth of flash and light,
says, *Honey, kitten, that's a hot town out there—let's
go cruise around somewhere and eat some sukiyaki*

This was, after all, 1980 in New York City
Nobody was sleeping. And everyone was feeling
lush and dangerous, and just a little Japanese

Blue Skies, Indiana

The anxiety of being alone disappeared this morning
Yesterday, it took twelve hours to travel from New York
to Indianapolis because of rain and wind and bomb scares
All on the same day. Can you imagine? God was unhappy
with the traveling public, I decided, as I meekly evacuated
O'Hare along with six thousand other passengers displaced
by a terrorist or simple lunatic who jumped a security barrier
Hours later, when they let us back in, I did not pet the bomb-
sniffing dogs and say, *Good puppy*, because working dogs
are known to take offense at any suggestion that they are not
serious animals doing serious work. God loves them, loves
all creatures who serve man or nature. Perhaps it was me
in particular that He (okay, or She) was angry at on Thursday?
And because you were not there to point out that this thought,
too, could be considered lunacy, I entertained it for at least
five minutes. Hence the anxiety? No, probably not. Panic,
for me, is something more philosophical. It is something
more deeply human. It has something to do with being alive

Which brings me to the point: I like to travel, but not alone
I fall asleep on airplanes and miss the meals. I have trouble
reading train schedules and get confused about time, which
apparently runs backwards and forwards and curves around the
earth like a bracelet of loose atoms sliding around a blue ball
Maybe that's it: separated from the few constants I believe in,
like the firm, familiar coast that reaches down to grip the bedrock
or the seasonal tides that bring the herring gulls and terns, I seem
to lose the markers that tell me who and where I am. I become

a gene pod, drifting on low-level winds, or the wind itself,
full of clouds and chemicals, with electrical impulses blinking
on and off like faint lights signaling disaster. Or maybe it's
actually a lot easier? Maybe I'm just lost without you? Which
could explain why I wake up thinking, *I am human. I am alive
I am alone.* But No, you whispered down the phone lines
in the morning. *Go to the window. What do you see?* And I
was able to reply, *I am under blue skies. I am safe in Indiana*

Oh bless you for reminding me. That I am not lost
That from here, even I can find my way home

WHAT THE DARK-EYED ANGEL KNOWS

A man is begging on his knees in the subway. Six-thirty
in the morning and already we are being presented with
moral choices as we rocket along the old rails, through the
old tunnels between Queens and Manhattan. Soon angels
will come crashing through the ceiling, wailing in the voices
of the castrati: *Won't you give this pauper bread or money?*
And a monster hurricane is coming: we all heard about it
on the radio at dawn. By nightfall, drowned hogs will be
floating like poisoned soap bubbles on the tributaries
of every Southern river. Children will be orphaned and
the infrastructure of whole cities will be overturned. No one
on the East Coast will be able to make a phone call and we
will be boiling our water for days. And of course there are
the serial killers. And the Crips and the Bloods. And the
arguments about bilingual education. And the fact that all
the clothing made by slave labor overseas is not only the
product of an evil system but maybe worse, never even fits

so why is it that all I can think of (and will think of through
the torrential rains to come and the howling night) is
you, sighing so deeply in the darkness, you and the smell
of you and the windswept curve of your cheek? If this
train ever stops, I will ask that dark-eyed angel, the one
who hasn't spoken yet. He looks like he might know

TAMIAMI/MY PAST LIVES

Well, I was not a priestess. I was not a prophet
or a Druid—I doubt that I even had a good job
If I ever get to tour any ancient outposts, it is unlikely
that I will bump into my own tomb or find
a rhodolite bracelet that some lovesick warrior
left beside my cottage door. Nope. I could hold a séance,
channel with an expert, and the most interesting thing
the spirits would report is that I once lived in a forest
with a relative who had a talent for hunting truffles—
and it will turn out that we were both afraid of hares
(they were bigger in those days and had longer teeth)
Even Seth, aswirl in mystic colors, could check
nine levels of higher consciousness and alas, find
little evidence of me: a comb, perhaps (I was always neat),
a leather shoe, dog toys (wolf toys?), a letter
to the local authorities complaining that lately,
they are letting the witches witch up too much rain

Let's face it, facts are facts and I am willing to own up
to mine. For a million years or more, I've been
uninteresting. If I've been appearing, reappearing,
as a girl, a boy, a shellfish when I was bad, a marigold, briefly,
in a walk-on for a week, then I've been a disappointment
to the ages. I'm sorry, Gucumatz, Anubis! I guess
I just didn't get what you were driving at with the
boat graves and the skull games and measuring
degrees of shadow east and west of the rising sun
But things are better now, here on the Tamiami Trail!

I mean, I'm really getting in the swim of things,
now that I've popped up in this sunshine paradise, this
shark's tooth capital of the world! How did we
miss this? I know time fears the pyramids,
but I'd like to be comfortable while time is stalking me

So send me back, boss, send me back!
Give me a luxury condo with a view of the
Inland Waterway (throw in a strip mall and a
golf course and credit cards with low APR)
and I bet you I could really get things
rock and rolling in this southern clime!
We'll call Highway 41 the road to revelation
and shoot those souls right down here to the beach
We'll have a party! We'll all be getting wiser!
Soon the whole world will be full of higher consciousness
and all because we eased up on the regulations
Forget sacrifice and monoliths! From now on it's
tee shirts and Ray-Bans for everybody. That'll keep us
coming back (and coming back) for more!

WHEN THE WHITE BUFFALO COMES

Let's say your car breaks down on a road outside of town
and you have to walk across a field of winter wheat to find
      a farmhouse with a phone
It's October, Halloween weather; crows streak across
      the darkening sky
Suddenly, you stumble into a ditch—only it's not a ditch,
it's a circle, wide as a skating rink, pressed into the broken crop
Three smaller circles surround this spiral: perhaps they are
the stars in Orion's belt, the three pyramids at Giza
As you rise to your feet, the farmer comes running, his wife
      in her apron comes running
and they tell you don't be frightened, this happens all the time:
Nine times out of ten, it's kids with ropes and boards
      and patterns copied from a book
The bent grain crackles, the wind rises in the lonely field
Yes, the wife says, as she leads you back to the farmhouse:
      nine times out of ten

Or you could be visiting a friend in an outer suburb
Let's walk over to Montgomery Street, he says
and when you get there, you see a young girl sitting
      in a chair
The girl is in a coma. Her family leaves her on the lawn
      like a flower in a pot
Soon her face swells up with ecstasy and though she never speaks
her neighbors gather with their opinions: *she sees the sun in shards,*
      she sees holy intervention
But these are not her visions. She is really dreaming

47

about everyone
She may love us. She may not

But this is only the beginning, how you happened on
            Khufu's footprints,
met a mystic in a dream. Years later, you are in a diner
            on the highway
when you hear a rumor that the white buffalo has been born
And since you never know and won't conjecture,
you tuck some crackers in your pocket to sustain you
            on the way
then head out to the spot where the nations have assembled
to see what next comes walking through the silence,
            down the road

Nirvana

I know that in the years to come there will be robots waiting to assist me
I know that there are quasars and pulsars broadcasting at frequencies
        that will change our minds about everything
I know that pearl divers will find antediluvian capitals
that will prove we knew more than we thought we did
        before we thought we knew anything
I am not afraid of religion or technology and am interested
        in cults of all kinds
I expect everything: doomsday, resurrection, cancer, Y2K,
        miracle serums, psychic revelations
I believe that immigration is both a boon and a bane
and that this is one world that should have one government
but accept that we will have to get rid of some of the bad people
        (and don't pretend that you don't know which ones)
I believe that language should be changed by the people
        who speak it, and am untroubled
when I turn a corner and find that a building I once lived in
        has been torn down
I am ruthless at my job, heartless in my judgments, but kind to pets
I believe that culture is what we make it and that the evening news
        is an auction of cultural souvenirs
If you buy this story, then we will sell you another
Me? Happily, happily, I buy it all

In effect, I have achieved Nirvana. I am of a time, a place
Perfectly suited to my environment, bred from my environment,
        definitely more nurture than nature, I cannot be hurt, abandoned
        or insulted

49

If I were, I would buy a book with handy tips on how to deal with
these problems

and I would deal with them. I am looking forward to the future.

I am full of joy. I believe that the stars are an infinite road laid out
for me to follow, that instructions

have been left for me, that I have been created to live here, now,
everywhere,

and to think about everything that has been brought to my attention

Watch me, watch me. I am not the first, I am one of many, I know
what I am doing

I am clean and sober and lean and ready. Bring on the robots.

I know they will be wonderful. They will do everything I want them to,
and do it well

TUCSON CHRIST

Tucson, Arizona, 1999

In Tucson, Christ is spare and narrow, sad as an Indian
in a Spanish landscape. He won't play golf, won't sit still
for a massage, and refuses all the Mexican jewelry piled at
his door. Instead, he sails down from the Santa Catalinas,
a desert rose borne by a desert wind, and floats above us
in the clear blue sky above the broken brown mountains,
whispering our names. It is so quiet here, we can hear him
land on his soft feet, healed these thousand years, hear him
as he walks among the cactus plants, which offer him their
yellow crowns of pears and flowers. *We are all Jews,*
he tells them as he climbs back on the thinnest cross
above the smallest adobe hut. *We are all still wandering*
And what else was he saying when he appeared above us,
bright as the high sun above the chaparral? Just *hello*
And we waved back, recovering from our own long
and troubled history. *Hello, brother. Hello*

ON BEING A DISPLACED PERSON
(NONYA IN PARIS)

It was not romantic, let me tell you
The city looked medieval, the Seine sometimes
       smelled like fish
And I didn't like the food. Of course I was tired
and worried, and I only had three dresses and
a black felt hat—nothing appropriate for July
July in Paris: I didn't see lovers, I saw refugees
       from the Balkans
We were the ghosts in the cafés, drinking coffee
with shaking hands, counting money in our heads:
       how many francs, rubles, dinars?
I believe there was a waiter once who spit in my cup
Actually, not so different from Moscow! Rude waiters,
       pigeons, dead-end boulevards:
These are my memories of how I spent my time
       after the fall of Communism
I waited, I wandered. I lived in a blank space, in the
       silence between an old life and a new

I had visa problems, but I was saved by faxes:
No airmail letters on crackly onion skin for me!
I put my dresses in a Fendi carry bag (of course
       a fake—what else
could you buy in any Russian city that last spring?)
       and flew away
TWA. It took me a year to save the money to buy
       that ticket!

On the plane, I made myself think in English
I thought: I ought to change the color of my hair
        (Ultresse, Preference:
I knew all the brand names). I was a blonde in a
        cold country on the edge of Asia:
perhaps a redhead in a land of warmer winds?
All the hours I was in the air were like stones
I was throwing back at Europe. The stones fell
        in the ocean. I never slept

Now I am in New York, working in my cousin's store
where we rent videos. These are the films that people
        ask for again and again:
Taxi Driver. Star Wars. Any new movie with Tom Cruise
My cousin gave me a map of the subway, a map of
        the buses
Does this sound better than when the Germans
eviscerated a generation and set the populations
        of the world adrift?
It is, I guess, but not by much: it's just postmodern exile,
        exile with airplanes and mixed drinks
You still wake up in the morning and don't know what
        the radio is saying to you,
always smell the sea although you're miles and
        miles inland
You'll never understand the history or the fashions,
        never claim the culture
You'll always be years and years behind the times

Last Easter, there was a priest in a church on
        Bakhrushin Street
who told me he thought that some of us are seeds

that God is sowing,
sending us from place to place in search of soil where
something He is dreaming can take root
And that is how I feel sometimes: hard as a kernel,
windborne, unborn, a redhead who was a blonde
in Paris,
a woman inventing the future, a girl of tomorrow,
a ghost, a dream, a thistle someone is holding
until someone else lets go

MAGAZINE STREET

The hotel stands above the great bend in the Mississippi River
Every morning they bring beignets with the morning news
I could sit at the window all morning, watching the barges navigate
the mud flats, watching the silt of a million years accumulate
in the delta. (In my mind, I see a satellite photo: levels of green,
levels of blue—and there is the delta, the stubborn river, the plague city,
recovered now, busy, hot as a star beneath its alluvial plain)
But it is getting late now, and I have business to do. I go
downstairs in an elevator with ruby carpeting, dim mirrors
I am ready to slay my enemies. To be formidable, a terror
In a satellite photo, I would be flame colored. I would
stand out like a hostage taker in a city full of victims.
Don't even dare try to negotiate with me!

Later, I go touring. I ride a trolley through the Garden District
where the Tulane students are washing their cars and thinking
about the law. Just as you would expect, the lawns are overgrown
with vines and creepers, even the trolley tracks have sprouted flowers
I buy a tee shirt in a candy store (*I love the Crescent City!*),
a Mardi Gras necklace of yellow plastic beads. When I
call you from a phone booth on the corner of Coliseum Street,
you are already laughing because you know it's me
So killer, you say, *are you missing me?*

Well, of course. I call you
from Jackson Square where bells are ringing
from the Café du Monde where I'm buying French coffee
from Bourbon Street, which I think is dangerous

from po' boy shops, where the chicken is extra spicy
from Galatoire's, from La Louisiane, from Algiers
On a satellite photo, my heart would be extra visible
like a piece of bright candy among the dreary isobars
My phone bill would be in a museum

So here I am at the city airport, loaded down with
a traveler's gifts. I have a harlequin doll, a souvenir mug,
a crawfish key chain, some potent ju ju in a jar
And I hope that you are ready when I get there,
when I'm transported from the Easy to the Eastern Jewel
I hope you're hungry and happy and in the mood
for fun—because I have been on Magazine Street,
home of the assassin, and I think I want to try a little
down-home magic, turn some evil into good:
On a satellite photo, you would see me on this airplane,
pulsing, pulsing, ready for anything but gunning for you

I Am Writing You Tonight

The fishing boat is coming home after traveling the wide ocean
It glides through the shallow channel beneath a silver slice of
    summer moon
The light is on in the wheelhouse and a friendly radio reports
that princely codfish have been seen sleeping in the inlet
    beyond the midnight shoals
And where am I? Watching from a bench outside a famous
    restaurant that sprawls across the pier
Inside, film stars and cinéastes are dining by windy candlelight
They pay with raw diamonds and are served with raw gold
    while the codfish dream of all of us
Their dreams are rumored to be luminous, like stars
    beneath the sea

and F., F., I am writing you tonight to say that I have no one
    to eat with, no one to sleep with
I hope that you have found safe harbor. I am still here, waiting
    for what comes next

PHYSICS

Let me lay out the choices for you, and you only
        get one:
Order, supreme and preordained, which you can
model with colored balls and sticks, which is
        inevitable and luminous,
eternal as a pyramid and a pyramid and a pyramid
and a pyramid on the endless plains of time—or
chaos, which is desire and depth, infinite depth,
        infinite smallness
passing through a wormhole to the other side
of a spinning, spiraling, white fire, blue fire,
        exploding galaxy
and coming out the other side in energy so ultra
violent violet that it can never be expressed
So pick one—and no looking at your neighbor's
        paper
Pick one now

And while you're choosing, this is what else
        happens:
In a classroom overcome by summer, a physics
teacher stands up from his desk and walks through
        watery green light
(light through leaves, through chalk dust, filtered by
        humidity)
to the front of the room. He says to the class,
I want you to think about this theory: that if something

is true, it should be intuitively obvious to the casual
    observer
What he means is that if something, at its core
    and in its essence,
is irrefutable and pure, even someone who is disinterested
in it (and *it* may be a thing or a hypothesis that is, or was,
    or may yet be)
should be able to determine the set of circumstances
that have given rise to *it* and predict their outcome
But the students are outraged. *That isn't physics*, they
    cry out,
That is philosophy, and they all march off to go surfing
The teacher doesn't care. The teacher is a substitute
He has his own dreams

This is also what happens: My companion, X and I,
are walking in Griffith Park, near the observatory
X is weeping. X may be weeping because of some
    personal distress
or because so many more acres of the rain forest have
    been denuded
(X has many fears and wide-ranging concerns)
But since I haven't asked, the cause of X's pain is
    undetermined
I, personally, am waiting for news from the observatory
I have been waiting for this news since I was a child
My anxieties, which rival X's in complexity, are
soothed by the thought that telescopes are searching
    the universe, always on alert
I remember the day I read about the Very Large Array:
I felt like I could breathe again, that finally, there was

a chance to gather data by which something important
          might be explained
But here is the problem: X is inconsolable. Can we use
any of the information here to determine the speed at which
          X's tears are falling
or how many eons it will take for X to cross Griffith Park?

Now let's go back, for a moment, to the physics teacher,
          the one with dreams
What is he dreaming now? Pure science, pure physics
(his students should have stayed—they would have
          learned a lot. The teacher
is a brilliant man). There is another theory that concerns
him: the one that suggests *sensitive dependence on*
          initial conditions,
which proposes that even very small actions can have
very big effects—which should be intuitively obvious
to even the casual observer (*now* are you getting this?)
The teacher, whose name is Y, stands up again: his intention
          is to leave the classroom and go home
Instead, he picks up an object from his desk (any object;
you may insert the name here _____) and hurls it through
          the window
While the sound waves from this event are just beginning
their infinite journey through time and space, the teacher
          waits in the empty room,
in the watery green light and wonders what will happen next
He is thinking, *pick one. Pick one now*

Meanwhile, X is still weeping. And the observatory, as yet
          has nothing to report

If Time Is an Engine

There are sunflowers on the path where I go
and lacewings rising from the fields
With each step I take, I know more surely
that this is the way

If time is an engine, then it was created in a dream
If love is an engine, then the dreamer weeps
If memory is an engine, then it will carry the dream away

But there are sunflowers on the path where I go
and the dog is at my heel. There is a gate
and a meadow beyond. There is a stream

The sky is blue by day, blue in the evening
but I know the way of the hidden stars
and I'm still alive, I still know secrets
There is nothing I have left undone

So my keys are on the table. You can sell my
clothes. Rust, rust is affecting the machinery
But I am not needed. The machines can be repaired

For if time is a cathedral, then I have lived in the cathedral
If love is a cathedral, then I have lived in splendor
If memory is a cathedral, then I remember everything

but now pass by. And there are sunflowers
on the path where I go. The dog is at my heel

There is a gate and a meadow beyond
There is a stream

ONE NIGHT IN THE 7-ELEVEN

One night in the 7-Eleven
(10 p.m., summer, Hopelawn, New Jersey)
I take my bottle of Fruitopia up to the counter
and make an impulse purchase of two
chocolate-covered cherries (one for me,
one for the spoiled dog), and then,
after I've paid and turned to leave the store,
I see the moon framed in the front window,
wearing a big, white, shimmering, beaming,
happy-go-lucky 1940s kind of face,
looking in at me, my dog and my
bottled beverage. It's so low on the
horizon, it seems like it's getting ready
to come in and buy some treats

Then I have this vision: children
all over the world, seeing this
giddy satellite, sit down at their
desks and write to famous astronomers
They want to know how far away
they are from this crazy moon
Children, children, the astronomers
write back, don't worry about the moon
The moon is too busy to bother you
It has to pull at the tides
It has to keep adjusting the sky's
dark blanket all around itself
so sometimes it appears to be a

crescent, sometimes half an orb
The moon has to renew itself: that's
why it goes away sometimes, to rest

So the children are comforted
But what about me? When I leave
the store, the moon follows me home
The dog barks at it to chase it away
But the moon won't budge
Moon, June, croon, spoon
Later, when I go to bed, I can still
see it in the bedroom window
It gets smaller and smaller as the
night moves on. The dog, thinking
she has won this battle, stretches out
on the rug and goes to sleep
I sit up for hours, watching the moon
drift further and further away
I feel that I should wave good-bye
because it's still smiling, still happy
even though dawn is about to raise the
golden curtain that will separate us from
each other, and all of us from our dreams

Eleanor Lerman was born in the Bronx, New York, in 1952. In the 1960s, her family moved to Far Rockaway, a beach community that had seen better days. The broken promises of postwar urban life and the isolation of living on a desolate shore still inform her work today. She is the author of two previous books of poetry, *Armed Love* (Wesleyan University Press), and *Come the Sweet By and By* (University of Massachusetts Press). Her short stories and poems—including a series on T. E. Lawrence—have appeared in such publications as *Christopher Street* and *Chicago Review*. She has been nominated for a National Book Award, received the inaugural Juniper Prize from the University of Massachusetts Press, and was the recipient of a fiction grant from the New York Foundation for the Arts. She lives and works in New York City.